MAY 30, 2022

I got the part.

From the time I was 22, I had always anticipated that
it would happen. There were numerous callbacks,
nail-biting moments, and sometimes feelings of dread.
Forty-four years passed and I turned 66 without getting
the role. Then the phone call came. The final callback. It
was official. I had breast cancer. My journey as a breast
cancer survivor began. A new role for me. While always
expected, the part was something I truly didn't want. For
the next nine months, I followed my oncologist's extraor-
dinary direction and played my part according to the
script. Five years later, I was able to take a bow.

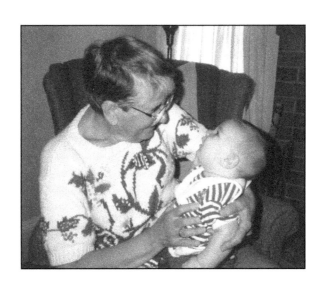

First in the Family

At age 52, my mother was first. Her cancer diagnosis foretold the future for other family members. Two of her three sisters followed with breast cancer diagnoses and, 44 years later, my Triple-Negative Breast Cancer was diagnosed. My mother certainly didn't know that she would live 23 more years to age 75, witness the joy of my pregnancy, and get to know our son in the first year of his life.

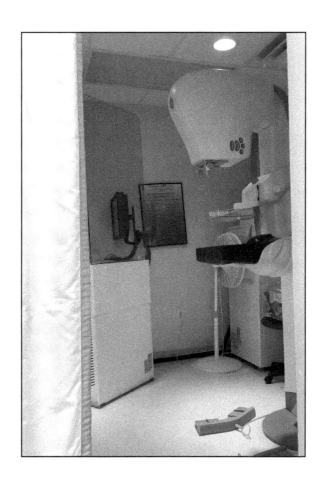

Last Callback ~ First Photos

I remember my first mammogram. I was 30 years old. Stripped to the waist and covered by a hospital johnny, I waited in the dressing room while the on-site radiologist reviewed my images. I wanted to hear, "All set. See you next year." Instead I heard, "The radiologist requests another image."

Year after year, I assumed that mammography callbacks indicated radiologists' caution because of my family history of breast cancer. I passed age 52, my mother's age when diagnosed, thinking that I had dodged a bullet.

The callback decades later didn't surprise me. What surprised me was the rather large white blob on my mammogram. I waited in the room for the radiologist's conclusion and took an iPhone photo of my surroundings to stay calm. Little did I know then that I would choose photography to document the next nine months of my journey.

Preplanned Visit ~ Unplanned Biopsy

Who would have thought I would be scheduled for a biopsy during our son's visit for a long weekend. If he hadn't been home, I would have waited for the test results—ever hopeful that there wouldn't be a problem and I wouldn't have to worry him. Because I was scheduled for a biopsy the morning after he arrived, I had to share the news. Looking back at this photo of me tells the story of the stress I was under. But to have my son Tyler at home was joyful and a much-needed distraction. The balance of yin and yang promotes a good state of physical and emotional health.

Triple-Negative was not in my vocabulary.

I've always been a glass-half-full person, a Pollyanna type. In spite of my past positive outlook, my current biopsy results revealed that I had TNBC, Triple-Negative Breast Cancer, a rare form of aggressive cancer with a high recurrence rate greatest within the first three years. There's a sharp reduction in recurrence after five years. Now that I've celebrated five years cancer free, I feel pretty darn good about my journey. I lived each day to its fullest and remained positive. Always positive. What's the alternative? Definitely not negative, especially triple-negative.

Controlling one small facet of my world with three lines

Waking up the next day after fitful sleep, I felt an entirely new level of anxiety. I had heard my diagnosis loud and clear. I understood it. I just didn't want it to be true. I've never been one to wait for things to happen. At that moment, I had no control over the process ahead or the outcome. I was inspired to write a haiku.

I've always felt in control of my life and this was a very new place to be. Writing those simple three lines with the five-seven-five-syllable structure focused my thoughts and emotions. The process allowed me to manage one small thing when everything else around me was unknown.

Keeping a promise
To be as strong as I can
Not sure how I will

Wake Up Call

Our home is directly across from a church. The bells ring their call to service every morning at 7:45 and again at 8:00 to welcome parishioners.

Clang of the church bells
Waking me to face the day
Bells don't drown the fear

In the midst of everything, our dear dog Denver declines.

At first, my husband Ron and I thought Denver, our 16-year-old Tibetan terrier, might be reacting to our state of anxiety. As the days went on, he stopped taking his meds even if they were hidden in ice cream. I asked our vet if we should increase Denver's medication dosage. Her response was, "If he's refusing to take his pills, more pills won't help. He's trying to tell you something." With great sadness, we took her advice to put him down. As much as we mourned his passing, both of us agreed it would be tough for us to juggle Denver's routines with all the treatments I would be going through. We were thankful that he and our veterinarian made the decision for us.

Our doggie Denver
Will always be on our minds
Always by our sides

Calling All Doctors ~ No Promises Made

When faced with a diagnosis like mine, anyone would be overwhelmed. I needed to make decisions quickly. Having moved to the south coast of Massachusetts just four years prior to my diagnosis, neither Ron nor I knew any surgeons in the area. We reached out to friends old and new and found two surgeons to consult, one locally and one in Boston.

Local

The first stop was to our local hospital where I had my biopsy. The surgeon answered our many questions. The answer he gave about how long I'd be hospitalized after a bilateral mastectomy threw us for a loop. He said, "DAY SURGERY!" Very quickly, we put all our eggs in the Boston basket.

Boston

The Boston surgeon had excellent credentials and reassuring answers to our questions. Surgery was set for September 12. Wait! That was just two and a half weeks away from the Philadelphia wedding of my dear friend's younger daughter. Could my operation be delayed a bit? As we were leaving the office, I asked the receptionist if I could see the doctor again to make a quick plea to push the date out. The doctor's response was an emphatic "NO!" I suddenly realized the gravity of my situation and it consumed me. Without missing a beat I said, "Okay, but make sure I'll be able to fly to Philly on Friday, September 30." She countered, "I make no promises."

Reality comes
Gathering information
I have a good plan

It's a Beach Day!

Ten days before my surgery, Ron and I hightailed it to our nearby beach. September is one of the best beach times after the summer crowds have left and taken the humidity with them. Kids are back in school. We arrived at a deserted beach and enjoyed abundant sunshine surrounded by white, autumn-like clouds. My kind of weather—warm days with cool nights. Weatherwise, Hurricane Hermine threatened our upcoming week, but I chose to soak up the sun with joy!

Beautiful beach day
Anticipating Hermine
Calm before the storm

FREE Advice!

An Earful

It seemed like everyone knew someone who had been through breast cancer—they wanted to share that their friend, niece, cousin, or aunt would be happy to talk with me about it. They were well-intentioned, but during one conversation with a breast cancer survivor, it was like a dam burst. This woman spoke for almost 35 minutes without taking a breath. She filled me in on her every discomfort and every emotional meltdown. My husband who was within earshot mouthed the words, "HANG UP!"

I was thankful, however, for those who told me, "Do not go on the internet for information. Only rely on your doctors for accurate information." As I learned more about Triple-Negative Breast Cancer, I focused solely on my doctor's advice.

People want to share
Their experience is not mine
Not helpful to me

TO DAY is the
To Morrow
that worried you
YESTERDAY
and All is Well

A Simple Cross-Stitched Proverb

As the day of surgery drew near, I found myself unraveling. I drew strength from this cross-stitched plaque my mother created when she was young. It hung in a prominent spot in my house and had always been a go-to saying for me. It has proven to be truly great advice innumerable times. I tried so desperately to once again draw upon the strength of those simple words.

Jitters have arrived
Difficulty focusing
Won't change the outcome

My way

Ron's way

There's no one way to do anything.

I tried to anticipate what I might not be able to do after surgery, such as tying back my hair with a banana clip. Enter my husband. As you can see in the photos, both Ron's and my methods secured my hair. I was beginning to let go of control and learning that hairdos really don't matter. Having a loving spouse, a caring relative, or a devoted friend to help is what truly counts. My hair clip might not be put on exactly the way I wanted, but like so many other things, it mattered not.

Waiting is the worst
The day after tomorrow
What hell awaits me

It won't be long now
Surgery will be over
Hoping for good news

(day before surgery)

The Plan for Drop Off and Pick Up

Friends and family came to the rescue. A longtime
dear friend agreed to drop Ron and me off at the hotel
closest to the hospital. We planned to take a cab to the
hospital early the next morning. Two days after surgery,
a childhood friend would pick us up and bring us home.
My niece was scheduled to arrive on Friday and stay until
Sunday when my sister would arrive to be with me for
the next week.

My Friend's Recollection of the Afternoon Drive to Boston

"I arrived to pick up Ron and Leslie. She was sitting at the
kitchen table balancing her checkbook. I was amazed.
But that's Leslie. Always focused. She even made a
reservation for the three of us to have an early dinner at a
restaurant just across the street from the hotel where they
were staying. I thought it was incredible Leslie had an
appetite. My stomach was in knots."

(day of surgery)

Fear Disguised by Calm Resignation and Hope that a Sentinel Watches Over Me

The hotel alarm went off at 4:30 a.m. A cab took us to the hospital for 5:30 a.m. check-in. The intake person told me she'd never seen anyone so calm, cooperative, and coherent. I must be a good actor because I was truly scared out of my wits. Who wouldn't be?

After my intake session, I was whisked to another building to have a sentinel node injection. Radioactive dye was injected into my right breast, the one with the tumor. This dye would travel through the lymphatic system, guiding my surgeon to the three nodes that would be removed during surgery. Pathology would determine if the cancer spread from the primary site.

A sentinel is a soldier or guide whose job is to stand and keep watch. That morning, I hoped I had someone watching over me from above. Prayers were plentiful from family and friends.

My last words to my surgeon as I was wheeled to the operating room were, "Don't forget. I have to fly to Philadelphia for a wedding in just 18 days!" I remember very little else about that day.

I didn't feel that calm
But I cooperated
I was coherent

(day after surgery)

Room with a View

I woke to this sunrise and the parklike setting across the street from the hospital. I survived the surgery. I was hopeful the cancer had not spread from the breast to the lymph nodes. The pathology report would be available in five to seven days. Waiting is the worst.

Window with a view
An arborist's dream come true
Beauty to behold

I had no chest pain, but I had quite a bit of pain in my upper left back. I couldn't get comfortable. The nurse said this was common. She placed a pillow under my left shoulder. Later in the day, two dear friends came for a visit. I wasn't myself. I practiced walking up some stairs with the physical therapist. When I returned to the room, I was overcome with sadness and I burst into tears. After my friends left, I was alone with my thoughts.

Welcome visitors
Old friends are the very best
Couldn't live without them

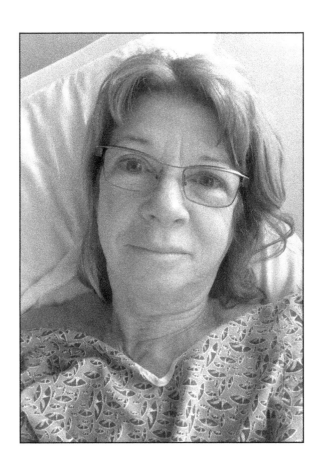

Homeward Bound

Going home today
Get to sleep in my own bed
Joyful occasion

Bye Bye, Breasts

I was never a busty woman and breast size never mattered
to me. Women today have greater choices when it comes
to surgery and treatments: breast conserving therapy,
mastectomy alone, mastectomy with reconstruction. For
me the choice was simple. My mantra throughout those
numerous callbacks after my mammograms was, "If I'm
ever diagnosed with breast cancer, I will have bilateral
mastectomies." It was a personal choice and one that
every woman should make for herself.

Home at Last with Family and Friends

Friends make it all right
Standing by to help you out
Asking for nothing

"Make new friends but keep the old. The new ones are silver; the old ones are gold." My oldest, dearest childhood friend brought me home from the hospital. My mother often said, "At the end of your life, if you can count your true friends on one hand you've lived a good life." People have hundreds of friends on Facebook and other social networking platforms. Everyone knows the ones who will arrive at your door if you're having a crisis at 2 a.m. I'm not at the end of my life, but leading up to my surgery and over these past several years, I recognized I have lived a very good life. I have a handful of true friends and for that I'm grateful. My mother would be proud.

Childhood friend in charge
I feel safe, loved, and cared for
Great she's by my side

Flower Power

I can't think of a better way to brighten someone's day than with a bouquet. From my first day home from the hospital until my last treatment, I had fresh flowers in the house. The first arrangements flew to my door in abundance. There was one very special individual, a former boss, who sent me a floral arrangement every week during radiation treatments until my last session on May 30. Remembering his thoughtful gesture to keep my spirits up still brings me to tears of gratitude.

Flowers aplenty
An expression of caring
Abundant with love

Family

In the early years of our lives, my sister and I grew up in
a three-decker, a popular house style in New Bedford,
Massachusetts. My Portuguese grandmother and two
maiden aunts lived on the first floor. My parents, sister,
and I lived on the second floor. The third floor was rented
out. I was very fortunate. I had loving parents who gave
me unconditional love. I've always said I could murder
someone and my mother would claim that I had been
provoked. My parents instilled in us solid core values.
"Do the right thing." These four words shaped my world.

My niece arrived.

I was so grateful to have her by my side. As always, she
was a calming influence. I came home with two drainage
tubes inserted under my skin in the areas of my surgical
incisions. These tubes were connected to two pouches
that collected the fluids. I was given a camisole with two
pockets where the two plastic pouches were held. Each
day, my niece meticulously kept track of the fluids from
my drains. When the drainage was less than 30 milliliters
in 24 hours for two days, the drains would come out. It
was a comfort to me for her to take charge.

How can I not hope
Positive thoughts surround me
Good news coming soon

The Phone Call

Ron, my niece, and I were seated at the kitchen table when the surgeon called late in the day to share the pathology report. Not the news I wanted. The cancer had spread and that news was my nightmare. My thoughts went to a dark place. I couldn't focus on much else.

The Pathology Report and Surgeon's Recommendation for Treatment

- Left breast clear
- 2.2 cm tumor in right breast
- Confirmed Triple-Negative diagnosis
- Margins clear
- Two of three lymph nodes clear
- Early stage 2B
- Recommendation: chemotherapy as well as radiation on chest wall and the affected lymph node site

Ron and my niece heard the news as positive. Two of three lymph nodes were clear. All I heard was that the cancer had spread to one lymph node. They also heard that the margins were clear. That sounded so good, but I thought if all margins were clear, why was there one lymph node that wasn't? Where was that random lymph node and are there more? Just one, I know, but that didn't sound good to me.

My mother had two radical mastectomies: surgical procedures involving the removal of the breast, underlying chest muscle, lymph nodes. I wished I had told my surgeon to remove my lymph nodes, but that was then and this is now. When I questioned my surgeon about not removing the lymph nodes, she shared that research has shown that women who have had radical mastectomies often suffer from lymphedema. This is a build-up of lymphatic fluid in fatty tissue under the skin. Lymphedema causes swelling and great discomfort, and it is incurable. To that I say, "While lymphedema is painful, it won't kill me. Cancer cells in the lymph nodes could." However, I bowed to the research with trust in my surgeon's knowledge and expertise.

No news is good news
Especially when it's not
Lymph node has cancer

SEPTEMBER 18, 2016

Changing of the Guard

*Portuguese women
Cry a lot, care a lot, too
Bad day yesterday*

This photo was taken the day my niece prepared to leave
and my sister arrived. I was blessed to have my sister by
my side. On this day of overlap, I enjoyed having both my
sister and her daughter keeping track of my fluids and
meds and generally fussing over me.

Whoosh!

The fluid in the drain is clear. Now, "all systems go" to remove drains. Medical procedures make me squeamish. The long drainage tubes just below the surface of my skin wound around in a random pattern. The thought of having them removed gave me the heebie-jeebies. I worried needlessly. I should have referred to my mother's plaque. The nurse told me to look away, take a deep breath, and then let it out slowly. Whoosh! Whaaat? They were out and I hadn't felt a thing. Now nothing kept me anchored at home. I'd been set free.

Last day of drainage
First day of freedom from drains
Beginning to heal

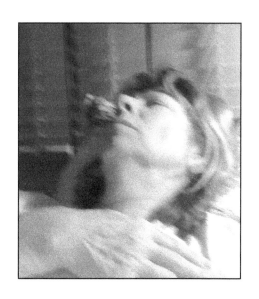

Just for the record, no one in our household was able to sleep.

What a Pain

Eight days have now passed
Not yet used to my body
Lie awake at night

PMPS, Post Mastectomy Pain Syndrome, is a relatively
common complication after breast cancer surgery that
causes chronic shoulder pain. I've never taken a lot of
medication. I was prescribed pain meds for the week
after surgery. I felt quite chipper that first week except for
the pain in my upper left back that I experienced right
after surgery. After taking my last pain pill, the back pain
problem intensified. It was relentless. I was fine during
the day, up and walking around, but as soon as I lay down
in bed, excruciating pain set in. What a pain it was!

Tit-less, sleepless nights
Will this pattern ever change
I really don't know

Eastern Medicine to the Rescue

Lights so bright, lights out
Night darkness doesn't bring sleep
Wakefulness persists

Looking to alleviate my pain, I surrounded myself with
pillows and tried sleeping upright in a chair. After two
sleepless nights, I reached out to the nurse on call. I
told her my problem and to my surprise she said, "You
shouldn't be having pain at this point." Not a good
answer. She offered to schedule a physical therapy
appointment the next week. But waiting was not an
option. I couldn't imagine making the trip to Boston. I
reached out to my local naturopathic doctor who came
to my home. Her Eastern medicine training rescued me.
Her healing hands were the perfect touch and provided
me with the comfort I needed.

A blanket of sleep
Swept over me in the night
Joyfulness at last

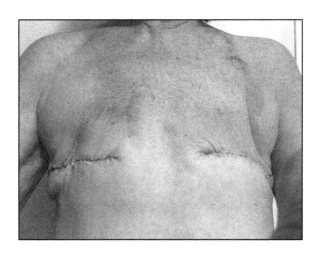

Lumps, Bumps, and All

Almost two weeks to the day after my surgery, I had
my post-op appointment with the surgeon. I arrived
with a list of questions related to the pathology report. I
had other questions, but they were not on my list.
I wasn't sure I'd be comfortable asking them. I questioned myself, "Would it be frivolous to ask about my
physical appearance?"

My body wasn't perfect to begin with and I'm not vain.
I didn't plan to run around topless after surgery. For that
matter, I never ran around topless before surgery. But
between surgery and my post-op appointment, I spent
a fair amount of time looking at my newly configured
chest. There were bothersome inconsistencies between
my right and left sides and I concluded that I should
definitely ask questions about my post-op appearance.

Questions from me.
Answers from my surgeon.

Was there another surgeon who operated on my left side, the one without the cancer? It's smooth and flat.

I was the only surgeon.

Why is there a hanging pouch on my right side where the cancer was?

When a patient requires radiation, there can be a tightening of the skin so there deliberately was more skin left on that side.

Why are there lumps on my right side above the incision that protrude and show through tops I wear?

Inconsistencies exist between duplicate body parts.

The night after surgery I questioned the nurse about the pain in my back. She told me it was not uncommon, and she placed a pillow behind my shoulder to elevate me. Why then, when I called the nurse in your office about the relentless pain in my back after the pain medication ran out, was I told, "You shouldn't have pain now." She should have been aware of what had been described previously as a common problem. My naturopathic doctor determined that my scapula was out of place and was able to alleviate the pain.

I'm sorry that happened.

I know women who chose to have breast reconstruction after mastectomies and had plastic surgeons in the operating room. If a woman chooses not to have breast reconstruction, shouldn't she still be able to have a plastic surgeon in the operating room during bilateral mastectomies? Was that an option I could have had if I had thought to ask this question on the front end?
Yes, and you can still choose to have a plastic surgeon remove the pouch at a later date.

Plastic surgery
Why didn't I ask the question
Scarecrow with a pouch

My last question and the one that had the most satisfying answer was, "Can I fly to Philadelphia on Friday, September 30, for the much-anticipated and all-important-to-me wedding?" I got the green light! I was raring to go and I'm so very happy I went – lumps, bumps, and all!

Darting Off on a Shopping Spree – Not for Me!

Between my surgery and the wedding, I didn't have
time to research options for undergarments that would
accommodate my missing breasts. My solution was
to wear a camisole with pockets stuffed with cotton
batting to fill out the darts in my dress. Darts are folds
(tucks coming to a point) sewn into garments to provide
shape for a woman's bust. Clothes with darts don't work
when you're breastless. At my post-op appointment, the
social worker suggested I could purchase special bras for
prosthetics at Nordstrom. And then she declared, "What
fun! Your husband can take you on a shopping spree." I
don't believe she grasped the difference between light-
hearted banter and making a sensitive situation trivial.
Her frivolity offended me.

What's the Point?

After going through the motions of purchasing
prosthetics and the special bra to accommodate them,
I made the decision to go braless. I still have those
prosthetics in their pink boxes with a rosebud on the
side, but I have no further need for them. My clothing
purchases will be dartless forevermore.

Here I am at the wedding with
Ron and our son Tyler.

The Wedding I Couldn't Miss

My desire to attend the wedding of my dear friend's daughter, whom I've known since birth, was palpable. It was unthinkable that I wouldn't be there. Her mother and I are great friends and were business partners for many years. Our children shared the same babysitter and grew up together. Our families spent many holidays at their house or ours. I have always been a goalsetter, but setting a goal when you have no control of the outcome is always iffy. Even though I held out great hope, I put my goal out there on a wing and a prayer to anyone who listened. My prayers were answered.

An Itsy Bitsy Stretch

It's easy to talk yourself into just resting. As most of us know, sitting around on the couch bemoaning one's fate doesn't do much for a person's mental state or overall well-being. Prior to surgery, I followed a 25-minute yoga routine two or three times a week. I was a little apprehensive to resume the routine. Then I remembered my mother doing an arm-raising exercise after her two radical mastectomies. The exercises allowed her to achieve and maintain her full range of motion. She stood 10 inches from a wall, raised her hands to shoulder height, and crawled her fingers up the wall as high as she could while she recited the *Itsy Bitsy Spider* nursery rhyme. My doctor approved my request to start yoga again. It was just the stretch I needed. Namaste!

Sneak Peek into My Future

I had the first consult with my oncologist. Walking into the cancer care facility was a sobering experience. I exited the elevator and peered into the waiting room. I got my first glance at people currently going through cancer treatments: some smiling, some pensive, some withdrawn, some alone, some chatting amicably, some anxious. I was in the anxious camp. Although I was there just to discuss my treatment plan, I could already envision the stages I would go through and wondered how I would fare.

Cold Room, Cold Operator, Heated-Up Patient

Local Facility

Adriamycin, one of the chemo drugs I would receive, has been known to cause heart damage. Before starting chemo, I had to have a transthoracic echocardiogram to make sure I had no issues with my heart. I was able to have this test done close to home. It was my first bad experience with a medical procedure.

Enter Technician

No chitchat from this one. Just orders. "Strip from the waist up. Johnny opened in the front. Lie on the table." She left the room. Ten minutes went by. Room was freezing. I got off the table and huddled in a chair with my sweater tightly wrapped around me. Enter techie, who barked, "You should be on the table." "I was too cold," I said. My excuse fell on deaf ears. When I got up on the table again, she told me to face the wall. Without looking at my chest, she reached over my shoulder and pressed a wand with gel directly onto my chest. I asked if she was aware that I had bilateral mastectomies just four weeks ago. She left the room, then came back and said, "It's all right," and finished the test. She abruptly left after telling me to use the rough brown paper towels to "clean yourself."

Speak Out

I'm not one to stay silent if something is wrong, but at that moment I felt diminished. I left without addressing the way I was treated. When I got home, I called the facility manager and shared my awful experience. She apologized and said that there had been other complaints about this technician. She assured me that mine would be the tech's last interaction with a patient. I rested easier knowing that those who came after me would not have an experience like mine.

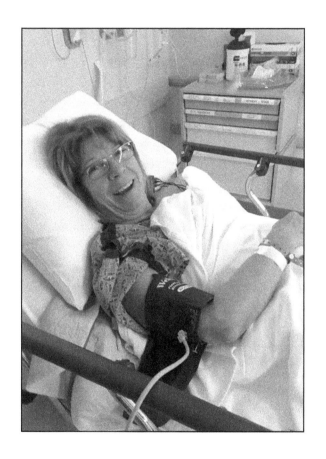

Any Port in a Storm

I had no idea what a chemo treatment would entail. All I knew was that I had to have a lot of them. I suspected there would be needles involved. I'm a fainter when it comes to needles, so a storm was already brewing in my head. How was I going to endure this? The oncology nurse provided me with the answer and calmed my anxiety. She said, "a port." It was a simple procedure to insert one that would allow the chemo direct access to my veins. No needle pricks! Calmer waters ahead for sure.

A port was put in successfully.

Two Days Before First Chemo

One last blast of sitting on the beach unencumbered by thoughts of what's to come in the next two days. Breathe in through nose; breathe out through mouth! Back to the message on my mother's plaque to calm me. "Today is the tomorrow that worried you yesterday and all is well."

And So It Begins

Chemotherapy Treatment Schedule

Adriamycin, Red Devil – *Once a week for three weeks*

Week 1 – **Thursday, October 20, 2016**
Week 2 – **Wednesday, October 26, 2016**
Week 3 – **Wednesday, November 2, 2016**

Taxol – *Every two weeks*

Wednesday, November 16, 2016
Wednesday, November 30, 2016
Thursday, December 15, 2016

Once a week for 10 weeks

December 21, 2016
December 28, 2016
January 11, 2017
January 18, 2017
January 25, 2017
February 1, 2017
February 15, 2017
March 1, 2017
March 8, 2017
March 17, 2017

First Red Devil Treatment

In the world of cancer treatment, Adriamycin is often called the Red Devil because of its bright red Kool-Aid color and nasty side effects.

My Nurse, Sheila

When I met Sheila, my oncology nurse, I gained immediate confidence that I was going to get through my chemotherapy sessions. I'll never forget her kindness, compassion, and caring ways. Seeing Sheila come my way with a smile on her face, hearing her ongoing reassurance that I was doing great, and listening to her encouraging words and bright outlook about my future was just the medicine I needed. Having her by my side for every chemo treatment was as powerful as the chemo itself. Never underestimate the importance of human kindness and interaction in the face of a challenge.

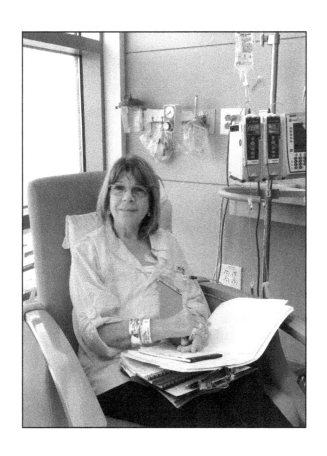

Always Be Prepared

First day of chemo. I have my questions ready, pen in hand. Information is power. Wearing the bright orange button-up-the-front good luck shirt my son sent me, I felt anxious but hopeful about the treatments ahead. I was in Sheila's good hands. Give me what you've got!

Cancer defines me
I will not let it be so
Hold onto the HOPE!!

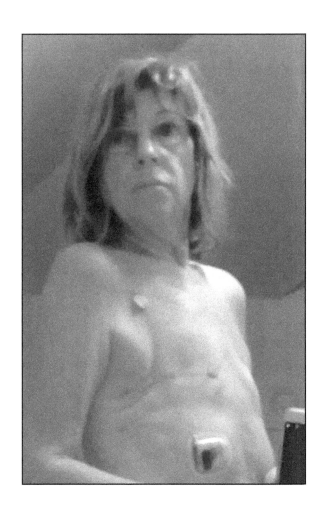

(late afternoon)

A Glowing Endorsement for a Glo Worm Experience

I was told I had to have a shot 24 hours after each
Red Devil treatment. This would have required me to
drive back to Boston the next day. Luckily, a Neulasta
patch, a new technology, was affixed to my abdomen
before I went home. Exactly 24 hours later, the device
glowed green. I felt a pin prick. As instructed, I sat still
for 45 minutes so the medicine could be injected into
my system. The soft green light reminded me of the
once popular Glo Worm, a preschool toy that when
squeezed would light up, creating a soft green glow. As
I experienced the advances of modern medicine, I was
aglow with joy.

I'm All Whipped Up!

Just four days after my first chemo, I was feeling great. How could I not feel great while eating one of my favorite desserts? Gingerbread with real whipped cream. I knew that there would be just one more Red Devil treatment after tomorrow!

Second Red Devil Treatment

I was raring to go and sporting a new hat with fake hair. While I had not lost any hair yet, I was anticipating it wouldn't be long before I did. I'm a planner.

Bounce Back

After each treatment I was tired, but amazingly I bounced back. I was entitled to have a day or two of feeling down. In truth, before every chemo session so far, I was on an up. My mantra after every treatment was, "I'm one step closer to having no more treatments on my agenda." Back to the beach for a calming effect kept me grounded. Just three more days and I would have my last Red Devil treatment! I was in the homestretch.

LAST Red Devil Treatment

My oldest, dearest childhood friend joined me for that
momentous occasion.

Cancer Clauses Herald Closure

Enter three Santa Clauses, now fondly called Cancer Clauses. These three endearing artsy figures got my attention in a catalog prior to starting my three Red Devil treatments. Always looking for some tangible element to measure my progress, I ordered them.

After each Red Devil treatment, I came home and raised the arms of one Santa. When all three of them stood tall with their hands up, I celebrated what I was told was the worst of the chemo. YAY!

Hair Today, Gone Tomorrow

OK, I'll just say this straight out. I've always cared about my hair. My hairdresser said she could help me transition to losing it. I decided to have my head shaved as soon as my hair began to fall out. On November 4, I woke and found a clump of hair on my pillow. I immediately called my hairdresser. Ron and I drove over for the shearing. I cried. A lot.

I sent a photo of myself to my sister when I got home. She agreed that I looked just like our father and we had a good laugh. While that wasn't a look I was hoping for, I felt his warm presence.

When I was young, I would check myself out in a mirror before leaving the house. My father always said, "You look like a million bucks." Not today, Dad.

Wiggin' Out

It took me some time to get used to being bald. I bought
into the idea of wearing wigs. They made me feel better
about myself but they had some inherent problems. I
have a small head so my wig tended to slip to one side or
the other. I could always tell when this happened because
whomever I was talking to would be looking at the wig
instead of directly at me. On the positive side, I once
had a compliment about my wig, or should I say, hair.
A stranger came up to me and said, "I love your hair!" I
was dumbstruck. Initially, I thought she somehow knew
I had had breast cancer and she was trying to be nice
to me. She genuinely loved my hair. When I told her it
was a wig, she was shocked. I didn't discount she was
an older woman whose eyeglasses might have needed a
prescription change. In any case, she made my day.

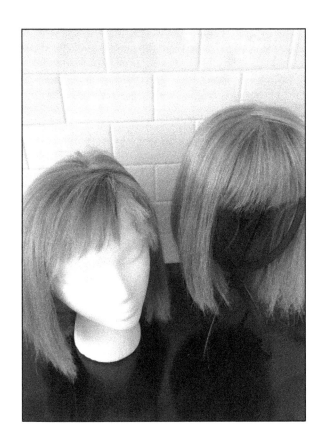

Identical wigs... but not anymore

Company's Coming. Keep Your Head Out of the Oven!

I've always loved to entertain friends in my home. I gauged my entertaining by the way I felt on any particular day. Invitations were impromptu. If I felt up to it, I'd invite people over. On this particular day, just as I was taking some stuffed mushrooms out of the oven, our guests arrived. They stared at the top of my forehead with a bit of horror. My bangs and the sides of my wig had fizzled up and dried out. Lesson learned: Never stick your head near a hot oven while wearing a synthetic wig. For that matter, never stick your head in an oven, period!

My first wig, the one on the left, is the one that had the unfortunate encounter with the oven. So I bought an identical wig, the one on the right. Luckily it never came within an inch of the oven. It is still a pretty darn good-looking wig.

Cool Head, Cooler Friend

I'm not sure how bald men survive the cold. I was freezing all the time. My college roommate came to the rescue with an unending supply of handmade, felted cashmere hats. So thoughtful, so comforting, and so very practical. Later on, she added some felted wool options that had a distinctive fashion flair. I loved them all, wore them all, and got compliments on all. I'll never forget her kindness in providing such a basic need – warmth.

Well into my treatments, my hatmaker friend came for a visit and saw me wearing my beloved hats. She confided that Ron had emailed her shortly after my head was shaved. Knowing she was a crafter, he asked if she could make something to keep my head warm. She replied, "I'm already on it." To that I said, "Great minds think alike."

The Best Hat Anyone Could Ever Want

Of all the hats my friend made, this was my favorite.
It wasn't the most fashionable one but it was the one I
loved the most. It was crafted out of luxurious cashmere
felted to perfection. I wore it constantly. Slept in it every
night. It was my magic hat. I wore it for every radiation
session. Keeping my head warm in that cold treatment
room was a godsend.

Back At It with a New Batch of Chemo

My niece came for a visit and joined Ron and me for my chemo session. On this same day, a longtime friend of mine moved into a home a little over a mile from where I live. I was itching to help her settle in. I have a knack for rearranging furniture and an eye for decorating. I knew she needed my help.

On the way home from my chemo treatment, I told Ron I wanted to stop at my friend's house. He was not in favor. He wanted me to go home and rest. My ever-practical sweet niece interceded and mentioned that decorating is something I loved to do and it would make me happy. We stopped and I directed the movement of furniture from room to room. After an hour or so of shuffling furniture around, everyone recognized that I was running out of steam. I conceded and went home. I felt exhausted, but good exhausted. Another chemo treatment down. A dear friend now living close by.

Down for the Count

Snooze Bucket

This evening found me shutting down... a real snooze bucket after a couple of busy days. In my eyes, a well-deserved rest. Let me be.

Up Again

A Pattern Emerges - Downs and Ups

"Ups and downs" took on new meaning during chemo treatments. My world was turned upside down, so why not turn this familiar saying downside up? When I went for a chemo treatment, I felt a little down but I knew that very shortly, I'd be up. Get the down out of the way and start moving up. Go with the flow.

A Reason to be Thankful Without Mashed Potatoes

Our son came home for Thanksgiving. We agreed it would be best to order Thanksgiving dinner from a local restaurant. Unfortunately, mashed potatoes were missing from our takeout meal. We got double green beans, but they weren't the best vessel for gravy. While it wasn't a traditional Thanksgiving, it was wonderful to be together and that was all that mattered. Later that weekend, we put up the outside Christmas decorations as we had always done on Thanksgiving weekend.

Fortify with
chicken soup

Take a rest

Happy to be
home

(chemo day)

Embracing a Routine

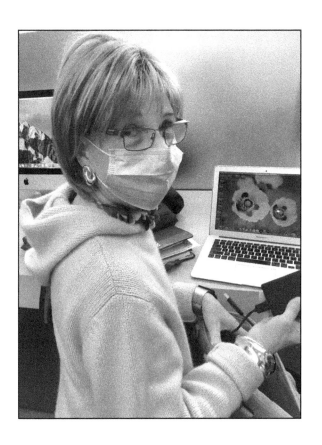

A Mask Before Its Time

My computer began to malfunction. It was traumatizing
for me to not have an online connection when I relied on
my computer to communicate with family and friends.
I donned my wig and headed over to the Apple store to
get my computer checked out. I was anxious about my
vulnerability so I wore a surgical mask to protect my
compromised immune system. It felt strange at the time.
Who knew way back then that wearing a mask would
become commonplace due to Covid four years later?

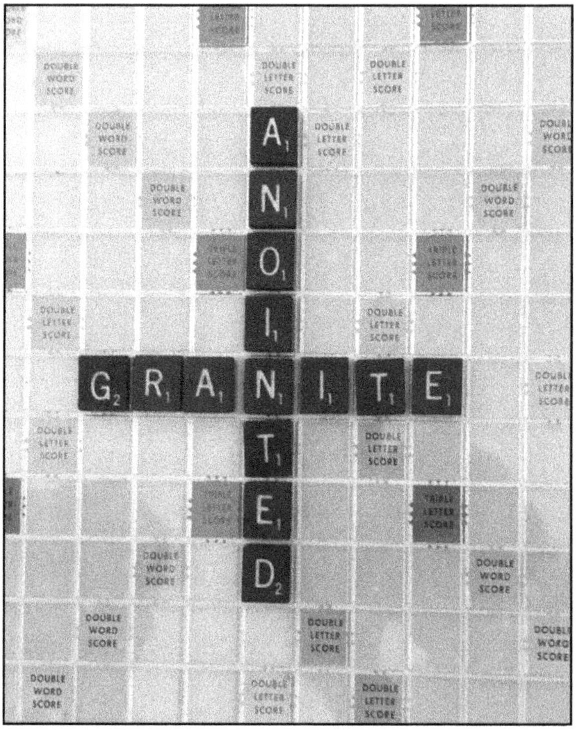
ANOINTED
GRANITE

A Joyful Occasion

Our son came home for Christmas. We played Scrabble.
Who has ever experienced seven-and-eight letter words
being played in the first two rounds of a Scrabble game?
Well, this photo documented that it happened. It was a
positive sign for me on two counts: the religious concept
of being anointed when sick and having a granite
constitution for the battles I still had to face. Being
cognizant of little signs the universe had in store for me
brought me peace.

Christmas Day

I have no idea what we ate or what gifts we exchanged, but I do remember we drove through Dartmouth into Westport and ended up once again at the beach. It wasn't a traditional Christmas for us, but it certainly was memorable. We got through it together.

Just in Time

My son gave me a pair of orange boots for Christmas, just in time for a major snowstorm. Much to Ron's chagrin, I decided to try out my new boots. I bundled up, went outside, dropped to the ground, and did what any other 66-year-old woman undergoing chemo would do... I made a snow angel just because I could.

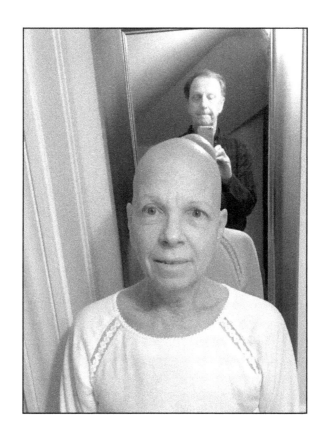

(chemo day)

Gumption

There were days when I looked in the mirror and asked myself, "Who is that?" This was one of those days. I got home later than usual from my ninth chemo treatment and I was tired. I was ready to go to bed when Ron came up behind me and took this photo. I suddenly remembered who I was: the woman who just three days ago had the gumption to prove that she still had what it takes to throw herself down on the snow and make a snow angel. Add to that, Ron reminded me that I only had seven more chemo treatments to go. Just for a moment I recognized the woman with the slightest smile staring back at me in the mirror.

The Women's March

Had I not been going through chemo, I would have gone to Washington, D.C. where I protested the Vietnam War on the Mall many moons ago. My son Tyler was well aware of my determination and my passion for women's rights. He was also well aware of my present vulnerability and was worried that I would go to the march in Washington where he lived. He called me a few days before and pleaded, "Mom, promise me you're not coming here for the march." I knew I couldn't make that trip, but I could go to Providence, closer to my home where I gathered a group of friends to stand up for Our Bodies, Our Business, Our Rights.

Spring Is in the Air

It was a raw winter day. I bundled up and went outside. To my delight, an early spring bloomer, a primrose, surprised me with its first blossom. It was nestled within a protected area of my garden where it got plenty of sunshine. I raised my face to the sky and felt protected, too. I've always drawn strength from nature.

Face Facts

During my chemo session, Ron and I met with a
geneticist. I didn't think there was any reason for me to
have the BRCA gene test until I learned from her that
our son could have a greater chance of getting prostate
or testicular cancer if I had the gene and passed it on to
him. She also said that although my mother and two of
her sisters had breast cancer, it didn't mean that I had the
BRCA gene. The most startling fact she shared was that
only 5% of breast cancer is hereditary.

I do *not* have
the BRCA gene!

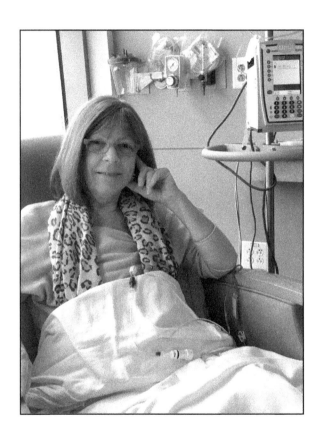

Only Three More Chemo Treatments

Last Chemo

Although I was overjoyed that my chemotherapy treatments were over, I was sad to say goodbye to Sheila. Anyone I've ever spoken to about going through cancer treatments cites their oncology nurse as their lifeline. The trust Sheila instilled in me started at my first chemo session and lasted until the end. I couldn't have gotten through it without her.

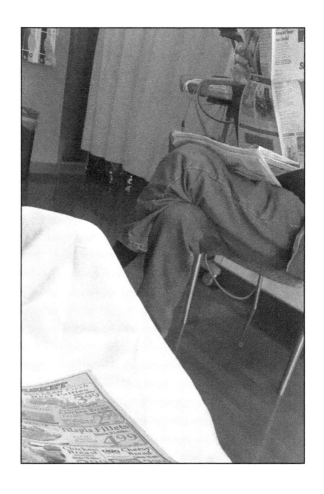

Treatments Became Old Hat

This photo brings back memories of my last day of chemo. It captured Ron and me casually reading the paper. We got through this together. One treatment at a time. What seemed insurmountable, downright scary, and sometimes never ending became a familiar routine.

Ron Was My Rock

I don't know how I could have gone through this journey without Ron. He accompanied me to every doctor's appointment and every chemo treatment. No matter what was going on, he was always there looking at me with concern. The sadness in his eyes reflected the sadness in my heart that I had brought all of this hubbub into our lives. Never once did he complain.

MARCH 18, 2017
(5:19 a.m.)

Now What?

No more chemo sessions. I thought I could relax a little, but my brain had a mind of its own. Why was I awake? I was thinking about my next phase of treatment: radiation. I started to obsess about everything. Why was my hand red? It felt like it was on fire. Was I starting to demonstrate signs of neuropathy? I worried about every nuance. The only remedy I had was my deep breathing exercises. Deep breath in through my nose, breathe out through my mouth. Repeat, repeat, repeat ZZZzzz.

Middle of the night
Darkness surrounds me with gloom
Morning light calms me

A Soirée on the Horizon

Looking ahead to an event on April 8, I decided to plan my outfit. A change of pace. A distraction. Good to feel good.

Should I wear my wig?

... or not?

Fundraiser at Our Local Theater

The wig won.

Primroses Aplenty Put a Spring in My Step

It's amazing what an early blooming flower can do to a person's view of the world. A harbinger of spring. Back in February, there was just one blossom. Now there are many. A breath of fresh spring air filled my head with thoughts of feeling well and drowned out the ever-present thoughts of radiation therapy commencing in a week.

You are the sum total
of everything you've ever seen,
heard, eaten, smelled, been told,
forgot—it's all there.
Everything influences each of us,
and because of that I try to make
my experiences positive.

Maya Angelou

Radiation Therapy Begins

My experiences so far had been positive, but I dreaded my upcoming radiation therapy. I understood why. When my mother had her first radical mastectomy, her only follow-up treatment was radiation. To this day, I remember her charred chest. Yes, charred. Blackened skin like a burn victim. She used to sit on the couch with a sheet covering her but not touching her. She ingeniously draped it over her shoulder from the back of the couch to the front of a strategically placed chair. Her intent was to keep warm and prevent anything from touching her skin in the radiated area. So, as I faced my radiation therapy, that image preyed on my mind.

Radiation Therapy Schedule

5 days a week, 6 weeks

Tuesday, April 18

Wednesday, April 19

Thursday, April 20

Friday, April 21

Monday, April 24

Tuesday, April 25

Wednesday, April 26

Thursday, April 27

Friday, April 28

Monday, May 1

Tuesday, May 2

Wednesday, May 3

Thursday, May 4

Friday, May 5

Monday, May 8

Tuesday, May 9

Wednesday, May 10

Thursday, May 11

Friday, May 12

Monday, May 15

Tuesday, May 16

Wednesday, May 17

Thursday, May 18

Friday, May 19

Monday, May 22

Tuesday, May 23

Wednesday, May 24

Thursday, May 25

Friday, May 26

Monday, May 29 (Memorial Day) – *a day off!*

Tuesday, May 30

Radiation Therapy Orientation

First Tattoo

As I mentioned before, I'm squeamish about needles.
I never wanted a tattoo. Little did I know that a tattoo
was in my treatment plan. I expected it would be painful.
It was not. Four small greyish dots marked the area
to be radiated and indicated where I could never have
radiation again. I was all for that.

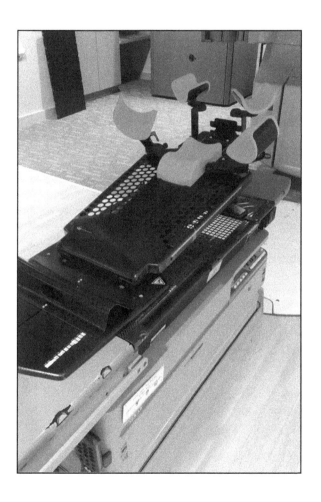

Get In Line

Getting lined up on the machine was a big deal. The radiation therapists had to make sure that the radiation would target where the cancer was located and not radiate any other part of my body. Stripped from the waist up, I lay flat on my back, arms over my head, my face turned to the left. The right side of my body would be radiated. The radiation therapists placed a device on my cheek that measured the tilt of my head and they made minuscule adjustments to reposition my head one way or another. They told me to hold those positions. The machine underneath me and overhead went one way and then another way, making creaky noises as it moved. I wanted to take my body off that creaky machine and get out of that room. But my role as the patient was to remain still. I was unnerved that no one spoke to me directly during the process.

Wait a Minute – More Information, please

I wasn't sure if I would receive radiation on my trial run day. As the radiation therapists began to leave the room, I called out, "Hey, hey, how long is this going to take?" They responded, "About 15 minutes." There would be no rays this day, just a positioning exercise. If I hadn't asked, I wouldn't have known, and believe me, that 15 minutes would have been interminable.

The radiation center had given me a squiggly wrist band with a hangtag on it to electronically check me in when I arrived for each of my treatments. At this point, my anxiety level was being stretched to its limit. On our way home, Ron and I drove by the beach just to calm my apprehension.

First Day of Radiation Therapy

Crying My Eyes Out – No One Noticed

It was an emotional day. I didn't know if any of the radiation therapists noticed that I was crying. I thought about my mother and remembered her radiation experience. I soon discovered radiation would be a totally different patient experience than chemotherapy.

The Difference Between an Oncology Nurse and a Radiation Therapist

Both are professional and both do their jobs well. This was my personal experience.

Oncology Nurse

An oncology nurse was assigned to me when I started my chemo treatments. I had the same nurse every time I went for a treatment. As a result, a natural bond developed. I trusted her implicitly. My chemo treatments took the better part of a day, so I was in her company a lot. Through numerous conversations, I learned about her and she learned about me. She became my friend, with whom I shared all my concerns. She knew what I was going through. She also knew all the answers to my questions. She explained everything about each treatment and told me beforehand what would happen on any given day and what I might experience after I got home. She anticipated and attended to my every need. She was my lifeline.

Radiation Therapist

With radiation treatments, no one radiation therapist was assigned to me. There were always two or three radiation therapists in the room when I arrived. I never knew who might be setting up the equipment on any given day. It was a stark difference from my experience in the chemo cocoon. But I understand that radiation therapists have a very demanding job. They have to make sure that everything is lined up perfectly and the treatments are timed properly. There's little room for error in radiation treatments. They have to concentrate on the smallest of details, leaving nothing to chance. Unlike spending the better part of a day with my oncology nurse, my radiation sessions took 15 minutes. Don't get me wrong, radiation therapists are very lovely people once you get to know them. Their focus is on the treatment, as it should be. It would be nice if there could be more personal engagement with the patient lying on the table. It would be comforting if they would keep the patient informed about what was going to happen.

From a patient perspective, I found the difference between the two experiences unsettling. However, I recognized that both were necessary and accepted them, differences and all.

Something Isn't Right

The second week, the radiation therapists I had become acquainted with were not there. Two different radiation therapists were on duty. Neither spoke directly to me. When they left the room, the machine was going in a different direction. The sounds were different. There were long pauses when nothing happened. I worried and began to think they didn't know what they were doing.

When they came back into the room, I put my arms down as I usually did after a session. They yelled, "Don't move! Stay in position!" I lay back down, unsure of what was going on. They told me they had done a test X-ray to make sure everything was lined up properly and that I still had to have my radiation session.

They left the room again. Uh, oh. They hadn't measured to make sure I was lined up like the other team did at the beginning of each session. I had moved when I put my arms down. They didn't put the measuring device on my face as the other radiation therapists. I worried that they might be radiating the wrong part of my body.

I have never been able to withhold my thoughts when I think things can be improved. I expressed my concerns to another staff member and asked to be informed about future procedural changes. She must have spoken to the staff because, after that, the radiation therapists were more communicative and informative.

APRIL 25, 2017

As Cold as Greenland

The radiation room was always uncomfortably cold. While the radiation therapists were fully clothed, I was naked from the waist up. When I expressed how cold I was, a blanket was finally provided for the lower part of my body. I asked why it was so cold and was told that the radiotherapy machine makes the room very hot so they have to have the air conditioning on. For what reason? The radiation therapists? The patient? The machine? Couldn't they provide heated blankets like those I used during my chemo sessions? They could not because they didn't have a heating device.

Get undressed

Put on johnny

Hang up wig
and clothes

Feeling cold

Put favorite
warm hat on

Get ready to lie in
the cage

Getting into a Routine

As radiation sessions went on, I got into a rhythm. One day I had straight radiation; the next day I had radiation with a gel pack on my chest. I was terrified of being charred like my mother. When the BEAM ON sign lit up and the machine whined on with loud, annoying sounds indicating I was being radiated, I memorized how long each radiation session lasted. I counted, "One, one thousand, two, one thousand... ," until the sign was no longer lit. It was comforting to me to keep track of the time each radiation blast lasted. I was able to calculate how much longer I had to be in that room all alone. I was overjoyed when my system of counting indicated my session was near the end.

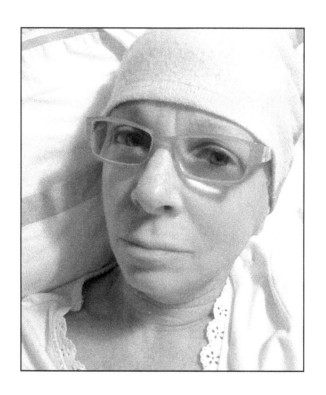

Already in bed. Miserable. I wasn't sure I wanted to go to our friend's Kentucky Derby party the next day. I'll sleep on it. We'll see what tomorrow brings.

Kentucky Derby Day

What a difference a day makes. I could have bet a million
dollars yesterday that I wouldn't go to the Derby party.
I was wrong. Every day is a new day. Each day presented
me with a new set of challenges and possibilities. That's
the way it worked. When I had a good day, I went with
it. When I had a bad day, I thought about the next day
being brighter. Don't count me out. I was still in the race.
One day at a time.

Not Wiggin' It Today

Emboldened and inspired by those Derby horses running like crazy, I felt I was getting closer to the halfway mark. The weather was warmer. I let my head breathe. I had some serious hair growth going on!

The Countdown

Five days a week for six weeks equated to 30 days of radiation. An hour and a half drive to the treatment center and back plus the 15-minute radiation session every day quickly became tedious. May 11, the day before my birthday, Ron shared with me that I was well over the hump—only 12 sessions to go. He cut up Post-It notes and placed them on our dashboard. For the remaining 12 days, they served as a visual cue that I was approaching the end of my treatments. The Post-It notes were a godsend.

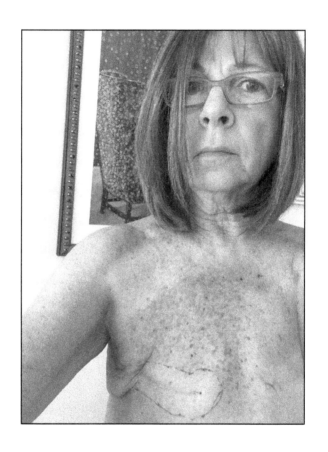

Zeroing In

As I neared the end of my treatments, the radiation therapists put a plastic shield on the area surrounding my tumor incision site and marked off the area where there would be the highest concentration of radiation for the final sessions.

Toughing it out

Common Sense Prevails

Things became a little dicey because the effects of the
radiation treatments were very uncomfortable. Staff
members suggested how I could care for my radiated
skin, but the information came in dribs and drabs. First,
I was told to do nothing. Hold off. Then I was given
an over-the-counter ointment which helped soothe
my skin, but I had to shower it off before going for my
next treatment. As my skin condition worsened, a staff
member said, "Oh, did I tell you about gel packs? Or,
did I mention corn starch?" No and No.

In the final stages of my skin irritation, I met a
knowledgeable, informative, and very compassionate
former nurse/technician who was filling in for
someone. At that point, I had some serious sores under
my arm and was questioning how I would go about
putting cornstarch in that area. I asked her, "What is
the best thing I can do to get through this experience
in the fastest way possible?" She offered, "Do nothing.
Sit on the couch with your arm up on a pillow and
let the air get at it." Bravo! My condition improved.
Interesting. My mother's history was repeating itself.

Dig In

Because Monday was Memorial Day, I got a reprieve. I was not due for my final radiation treatment until May 30. Almost there. One last radiation treatment. I kept myself occupied with the diversion of the day, digging holes for dahlias.

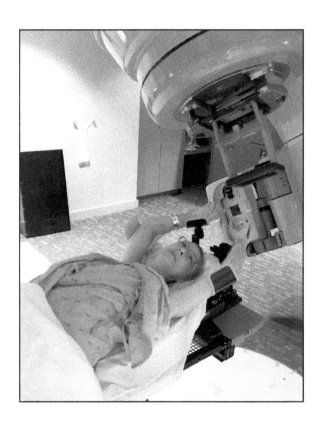

In the Cage for the Last Time

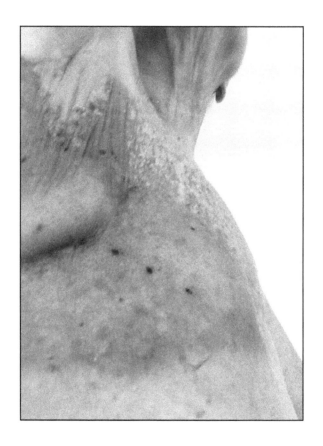

My Very Last Radiation Treatment

It was over. Not one more radiation session. I came home and, much like my mother, raised my arm over the couch to let air get at the right side of my chest and underarm.

My Day of Celebration – No More Radiation

The last beautiful flower arrangement awaited me at home. While I'll miss the flowers, I won't miss the radiation treatments.

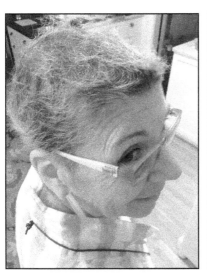 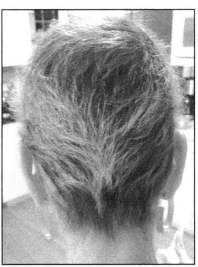

Accepting Where You Are and Loving It!

I never thought I'd love a hairdo like this one. I loved it
with all my heart. Ron frequently patted me on the head
and tousled my hair. These photos capture the disheveled
result. Yes, it looks goofy now, but at that time I was
feeling like my old self again. My eyebrows and eyelashes
were growing in, too. Now, I recognized myself when I
looked in the mirror. I looked like a newborn fuzzy chick
with a D.A. (Duck's Ass)

JUNE 14, 2017

Uh Oh! The Unintended Hair Debacle

I hadn't seen my hairdresser since November 4 when she
shaved my head. We met for tea. While we were talking,
she kept staring at my hair. Finally, she said, "Stop by
tomorrow and I can trim your hair. I'll clean it up a bit."

Before

After

Not Paying Attention

I love my hairdresser. When I arrived, she washed my hair. I sat in her chair, yakked my head off, caught up with her news, and shared mine. I didn't have my glasses on. I didn't pay attention to her snipping. When I got up from the chair and put on my glasses, I noticed that all my favorite fuzzy white wisps were on the floor. I held back tears and raced to my car. I sobbed hysterically all the way home. During my entire cancer journey, I had set goals, met them, and always felt I was moving toward being healthy. The new hairdo reminded me of the day my head was shaved. I tumbled back to when I wasn't well.

JUNE 18, 2017

Life Goes On

Most people wouldn't notice the difference and over the next few days, I became accustomed to not being a fuzzy chick. Considering what I had been through, the unintended debacle was a minor setback.

Follow Up and Follow Through

Just over a month after my last radiation treatment, I had a follow-up appointment with my radiation oncologist. I wrote a letter detailing my experience during treatment. I handed it to her to read later but told her the highlights in person. The points I made would not affect me, but I hoped that changes could be made to make things better for those who come after me.

Takeaway Message from My Letter

Put the patient first. Engage with them. Acknowledge they're in the room. Think about ways to make patients more comfortable both physically and emotionally.

It would be nice if you could bring patients into the radiation room before their sessions begin, explain the procedures that will be followed, and explain how long the process will be. Assure patients that while they may not be able to see the radiation therapists, the therapists can hear them if they have a problem. Information is power.

Note: My radiation oncologist reached out a couple of months after that appointment to inform me that she shared my experiences and feelings with the staff and my recommendations were acknowledged favorably. Not only that, the facility now has heated blankets for the patients. That gesture alone warmed my heart. She thanked me for my input. I thanked her for her willingness to listen to my concerns and make improvements.

MAY 30, 2017 - MAY 30, 2022

And so it is that
Life goes on
after breast cancer treatments

While I didn't take as many photos after my treatments ended, I continued to capture significant, feeling-well-again moments over the next five years.

A Family Gathering to Celebrate

Coming up on a year since my diagnosis, my family arrived to celebrate the end of my treatments. Family members traveled from Washington, D.C., Florida, and New York for a long weekend. They surrounded me with love and hope that I would get through the next five years cancer free!

Out of Town Guest Blows into Town... Again

A little over a year ago, these two friends had visited me in the hospital the day after my surgery. One came all the way from Maine. That meant the world to me then and more so now under such different circumstances. Instead of watching me walk up some stairs with a physical therapist, this time they joined me in a walk at one of my favorite places on one of the most perfect days in October. Sunshine on our faces. Sand in our shoes. We found another soul on the beach who took our photo, arm-in-arm, celebrating my recovery. I was back, new hairdo and all.

Standing Tall

A new year. A change of scenery. Ron and I traveled to
Scottsdale, Arizona. I shopped for some snacks for our
hotel room. I only needed a few things, so I grabbed this
small cart. Several people stared at me as I walked around
the store. I thought it may have been my wild hairdo.
When I got to the parking lot, I saw a child pushing a cart
just like mine enter the grocery store with her mother
who was pushing an adult size cart. Takeaway message. So
good to be alive and laugh out loud. Chalk it up to being
short. In my eyes, my cart was the perfect size.

Toy Fair at Javits Center NYC

Ron and I both worked within the toy and game industry.
We went to the New York Toy Fair show for many years
with the exception of February 2017, the year I was
preoccupied with cancer business. One year later, walking
through the exhibit hall, I had my super power back and
felt at the top of my game.

Bad Hair Day, But Who's Complaining?

Almost two years to the day after I had my last mammogram, I was once again at the beach. It may seem like I spent a lot of time at the beach. It's true. I'm a lucky woman to be living on the south coast of Massachusetts where I have access to several beaches. They've been a comfort to me throughout my journey. I can't explain the hairdo, but if I had to take a guess, I'd blame it on the humidity.

Winter Getaway to Florida

What a boatload of fun to get away from Massachusetts winter weather. I loved those spotlights on a series of sailboats outside of a restaurant where we dined. I couldn't resist shining a light on my good health. Ron obliged as he always did to capture a moment of happiness.

Out and About at a Local Fundraiser

The more time passes, the farther away I am from my treatments and the closer I am to my five-year mark. It's such a relief to feel well and to be out and about. To see and be seen. Smiles all around.

You Reap What You Sow

Every year I plant dahlia tubers by the end of May. They yield a spectacular display of gorgeous blooms from late August to the first frost. When I took this photo, I recalled the previous photo of me planting dahlia tubers on May 28, 2017. That was just two days before my final radiation treatment when I was at the end of my rope. Planting was a struggle, but I was determined to get it done. I persisted.

Just like the treatments I was plowing through, I hoped for good results. My dahlias never disappoint.

Reflections of a 70-Year-Old Mom

Today was my birthday ... a milestone one. I want to share a very natural emotion that a mother may have with her diagnosis. I was obsessed about the fact that I might die and worried how it would affect Tyler's life. At age 40, I was devastated when my mother died. I knew the profound effect it had on my life, and I didn't want Tyler to experience such a loss. Coming up on three years cancer-free, I felt confident I'd be around to see him for many more years. That assurance was a birthday gift to myself and a reason to celebrate with my son at one of my favorite spots on the shore.

Body Check

Looking at my body today, I recognize I would have benefited from having a plastic surgeon in the operating room during my bilateral mastectomy. However, it really doesn't matter what my body looks like now. Being healthy is all that really matters.

After all that I've been through, I still have a pouch! Oh well...

Closing Out the Year Feeling Healthy

In five months, I will mark my fifth year cancer free.

A NEW YEAR – A Special Celebratory One

Writing this book has been cathartic for me. I cried more while writing it than I did while going through my journey. It brought back sad and happy memories as well as some laugh-out-loud funny ones, too.

My photographic journey started when I took that first photo in the dressing room while waiting for my callback mammogram on August 9, 2016. I'm not quite sure why I thought to take it, but on that day, I had the premonition that I would never be behind a curtain again waiting for a mammogram.

I'm not a writer by trade, but when I looked at all the photos, I thought they were the basis of a story worth telling. I added text along the way, but the heart of the story is captured in the candid photos. I can see in my eyes the fear, the sadness, and the joy of coming up on my magical five-year milestone.

May 30, 2022
toDAY I Reached a major milestone.

5 YEARS being cancer free!

I'm a lucky woman! Lucky to be healthy and lucky to have YOU in my life. ♥

For All Who Bestowed So Many Kindnesses on Me

You may not remember the things you did to buoy my spirits, to calm my apprehension, to surround me with love, but rest assured, I will never forget any of them or any of you.

All the words of encouragement, the cards, positive sentiments, your willingness to be by my side before and after surgery, button-up-the-front pajamas, the numerous fashionable cashmere and felted wool hats, beautiful floral bouquets, orange balloons, delicious meals left at my door greeting me when I arrived home from a chemo treatment, a special orange vase, made-from-scratch chicken and turkey broths, Meyer's lemon cake, Mother Myrick's buttercrunch, special soaps, books, luxurious throws, to a knitted hat to wear to the Women's March sustained me and spurred me on.

You softened the blow of my ordeal. Today, I celebrate all of you for helping me reach this momentous milestone.

Remembering All My Hairdos ~ A Tale of Loss and Renewal

For most people, hair is an important aspect of their appearance. When a person needs a haircut or is overdue for a color treatment, he or she is likely to feel self-conscious or out of kilter. Almost everyone can relate to a bad hair day, but let me tell you, losing all of one's hair can constitute a very bad day.

Over the years, I had my brown hair dyed different shades, sometimes with an orange hue (my favorite color). I'd also had it highlighted with blond streaks.

When I lost my hair, I lost my eyebrows and eyelashes, too. This shook my confidence and self-esteem. I felt naked, ugly, and strange. Wigs, hats, and scarves helped, but they were poor substitutes for my own hair.

I was overjoyed when fine wisps of white hair began to appear in a random pattern on my chrome dome. Later, darker wisps emerged. The next aspect of hair growth was a bit unruly. I developed a collection of curlycues all over my head. They reached a length where I considered having them restyled a bit, but I ultimately decided to embrace all stages of new hair growth regardless of color or texture. My oncology nurse informed me that, after chemo, hair often appears curly at first but reverts to its natural state eventually.

She was correct. With length, my hair straightened out. However, the color remained black with streaks of gray. Salt and pepper. I love it and I love the fact that I no longer color my hair every four to six weeks. This was another cause for celebration. I'm enjoying my easy, breezy new hairstyle.

I invite you to view the following photos of my hair loss and regrowth.

A happy ending.

JANUARY 9, 2017   JANUARY 28, 2017   MARCH 3, 2017

APRIL 19, 2017   MAY 7, 2017   MAY 11, 2017

MAY 14, 2017   MAY 21, 2017   MAY 28, 2017

JUNE 2, 2017

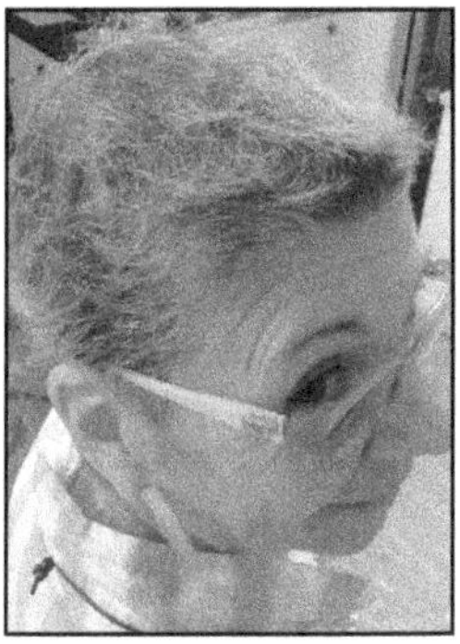

JUNE 2, 2017

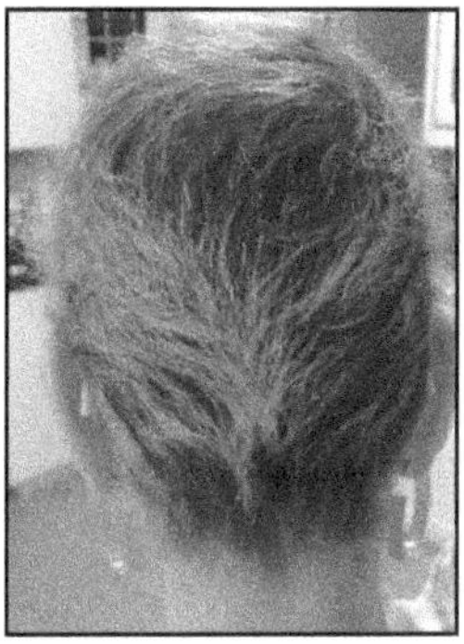

JUNE 4, 2017

JUNE 18, 2017

JULY 9, 2017

JULY 29, 2017

JULY 30, 2017

SEPTEMBER 8, 2017

SEPTEMBER 30, 2017

OCTOBER 23, 2017

NOVEMBER 11, 2017

DECEMBER 28, 2017

FEBRUARY 4, 2018

FEBRUARY 14, 2018

MAY 12, 2018

JULY 20, 2018

SEPTEMBER 8, 2018

NOVEMBER 11, 2018

DECEMBER 1, 2018

MARCH 3, 2019

MARCH 31, 2019

JULY 11, 2019

MAY 21, 2020

JANUARY 17, 2021

MAY 12, 2021

5 years cancer free!

afterword

So, there you have it. One woman's long journey through daily experiences with an invasive illness no one ever wishes to encounter, which unfortunately so many women do. From the beginning, Leslie had the wits and the drive to document her emotional and physical experiences throughout the long medical regimen by taking photos along the way.

As Leslie faced the five-year marker of her medical experiences, she was determined to add words to *I'm a lucky woman* and connected the photos with words that offered guidance, inspiration, and hope to fellow travelers on a similar journey. Woven into her story of chemo and radiation treatments are photos that captured events, support, and distractions that put her humanity into the prescribed medical steppingstones of breast cancer. There are many closeups of her at different stages. As I look at those many pictures of her at different stages of treatment, I see in her eyes and facial expressions different emotions of anxiety, hope, uncertainty, and yes, determination to face her illness head-on.

Somewhere in her memoir, Leslie commented that she did not choose the role she would play in the five-year journey. Elsewhere she cited me as her "Rock." It's not a role I would have chosen in a five-year journey, but I am only thankful and proud that in some small ways I was considered a rock in her story. The number one goal of her memoir is to give some strength and guidance to those who must face their own personal journey. That's Leslie, always wanting to be helpful to others with kindness in her heart. All who know her can attest, Leslie does have a big, courageous one. Certainly, so many small parts of the world that have been exposed to her are better places because she is a survivor!

Ron "the Rock"

acknowledgements

First, I wish to thank the handful of special souls, my family members and dearest friends, referenced in the book who took care of me when I needed them most. Know that I can never thank you enough.

I also wish to thank the people who were enormously influential in encouraging me to write this book. Their eyes and loving hearts were involved in getting this book ready for publication. From early readers to later proofreaders, I'm thankful to the following people: Anna, Barbara, Donna, Ellen, Hannah, Janet, Jean, Jessica, Joanne, Leslie, Loretta, Ruth, Marcy, Mary, Nancee, Nancy, Sara.

Special thanks to Ellen Gow, a professional editor, dear friend, and my felted wool hat maker, who weighed in from day one. I remember I doubted myself for thinking I could write a book. I sent her a text: You're the First One to Receive This. Her response to questions I posed was:

I thought I'd read a little of it before turning in for the night. Couldn't stop! Does it flow? It flows. Is it frivolous? Absolutely not. Too raw? Not at all. Too sappy? I did tear up when you wrote about Ron. It's your voice coming through 100% and that's what you want. I love it.

Ellen stepped up and shaped up my book big time. I will forever be grateful for her ability to make major edits while maintaining my voice. She threw every rule in the book at it along the way. And even though she tried to stop me from starting sentences with "And," I was able to sneak a few in with her approval.

My greatest influence was my husband, Ron. He read every word of every draft and it is his unwavering support of my efforts that has spurred me on to get my hopeful message out there!

LESLIE LAWRENCE often refers to herself as "a lucky woman," counting among her blessings a loving family and enriching friendships. Giving back to others has always been her life's passion. She retired early from the successful marketing company she founded to pursue that passion.

Undaunted by her breast cancer diagnosis, Leslie chronicled her experience over a five-year period with candid photos and heartfelt stories. The result is a revealing portrait of her triumphant cancer journey.

Leslie chose to give back once more and share her positive and hope-filled photographic memoir with readers. She and her husband Ron, who walked every step of the way with her on that journey, live on the SouthCoast of Massachusetts.

Follow her on Facebook and Instagram
and at *leslielawrenceauthor.com*

Printed in the USA
CPSIA information can be obtained
at www.ICGtesting.com
LVHW062322280224
773116LV00041B/2253